50 Iceland Main Course Recipes for Home

By: Kelly Johnson

Table of Contents

- Plokkfiskur (Fish and Potato Stew)
- Kjötsúpa (Traditional Icelandic Meat Soup)
- Icelandic Lamb Stew
- Hangikjöt (Smoked Lamb)
- Grilled Arctic Char with Lemon-Dill Sauce
- Pönnukökur (Icelandic Pancakes) with Jam
- Kjúklingur í Fati (Chicken in Cream Sauce)
- Plokkfiskur (Fish and Potato Mash)
- Lamb Shank Slow Cooked in Red Wine
- Pan-Fried Cod with Lemon Butter Sauce
- Fisherman's Lamb Stew with Root Vegetables
- Icelandic Fish Pie
- Baked Arctic Char with Herb Crust
- Lamb Chops with Rosemary and Garlic
- Grilled Langoustines with Garlic Butter
- Icelandic Fish Stew with Vegetables
- Braised Lamb Shanks with Redcurrant Sauce
- Pan-Seared Cod with Tomato and Olive Tapenade
- Icelandic Meatballs with Mushroom Gravy
- Baked Salmon with Honey-Dijon Glaze
- Icelandic Lamb Chops with Mint Sauce
- Slow Cooked Lamb Shoulder with Root Vegetables
- Pan-Fried Haddock with Caper Cream Sauce
- Grilled Prawns with Chili-Lime Butter
- Fish and Vegetable Stir-Fry
- Lamb Shoulder Roast with Juniper Berry Sauce
- Baked Cod with Herbed Crumb Topping
- Lobster Risotto with Saffron
- Icelandic Meat Pie
- Grilled Arctic Char with Mustard-Dill Sauce
- Smoked Trout Salad with Horseradish Dressing
- Icelandic Lamb Skewers with Yogurt-Dill Sauce
- Pan-Fried Haddock with Lemon-Caper Sauce
- Langoustine Pasta with Garlic and Parsley
- Lamb Meatballs in Tomato Sauce

- Baked Salmon with Roasted Vegetables
- Icelandic Fish Soup
- Lamb Loin Chops with Red Wine Sauce
- Grilled Prawns with Mango Salsa
- Arctic Char Fillets with Lemon-Herb Butter
- Lamb Shoulder Slow Cooked in Stout
- Pan-Seared Cod with Garlic Butter
- Icelandic Fish Sticks with Tartar Sauce
- Baked Trout with Almond Crust
- Lamb Burgers with Blue Cheese
- Grilled Langoustines with Lemon and Parsley
- Baked Arctic Char with Lemon-Herb Crust
- Fish and Chips with Tartar Sauce
- Slow Cooked Lamb Shanks with Root Vegetables
- Icelandic Lamb Stew with Barley

Plokkfiskur (Fish and Potato Stew)

Ingredients:

- 500g white fish fillets (such as cod, haddock, or pollock), cut into bite-sized pieces
- 500g potatoes, peeled and diced into small cubes
- 1 onion, finely chopped
- 2 tablespoons butter
- 2 tablespoons all-purpose flour
- 2 cups milk
- Salt and pepper to taste
- 2 hard-boiled eggs, sliced (optional)
- Chopped fresh parsley for garnish

Instructions:

1. In a large pot, cover the diced potatoes with water and bring to a boil. Cook until the potatoes are fork-tender, about 10-15 minutes. Drain and set aside.
2. In a separate large skillet or saucepan, melt the butter over medium heat. Add the chopped onion and sauté until softened and translucent, about 5 minutes.
3. Sprinkle the flour over the onions and butter, stirring to combine. Cook for another 1-2 minutes to cook off the raw flour taste.
4. Gradually pour in the milk, stirring constantly to prevent lumps from forming. Cook until the mixture thickens and becomes smooth and creamy, about 5 minutes.
5. Add the cooked diced potatoes and fish pieces to the creamy sauce in the skillet. Stir gently to combine.
6. Season the stew with salt and pepper to taste. Simmer gently for another 5-7 minutes, or until the fish is cooked through and flakes easily with a fork.
7. If using, add the sliced hard-boiled eggs to the stew and gently fold them in.
8. Serve the plokkfiskur hot, garnished with chopped fresh parsley.

Enjoy this comforting Icelandic Fish and Potato Stew with a slice of fresh bread or rye crispbread. It's perfect for warming up on chilly days and celebrating the flavors of Icelandic cuisine!

Kjötsúpa (Traditional Icelandic Meat Soup)

Ingredients:

- 500g lamb meat (such as shoulder or leg), diced
- 1 onion, finely chopped
- 2 carrots, peeled and diced
- 2 potatoes, peeled and diced
- 1 turnip, peeled and diced
- 1 leek, sliced
- 2 celery stalks, chopped
- 1/4 cup pearl barley
- 2 liters water or beef broth
- 1 bay leaf
- 1 teaspoon dried thyme
- Salt and pepper to taste
- Chopped fresh parsley for garnish

Instructions:

1. In a large pot, combine the diced lamb meat, chopped onion, diced carrots, potatoes, turnip, sliced leek, chopped celery, and pearl barley.
2. Pour in the water or beef broth, enough to cover the ingredients by about 2 inches.
3. Add the bay leaf and dried thyme to the pot. Season with salt and pepper to taste.
4. Bring the soup to a boil over medium-high heat, then reduce the heat to low. Cover the pot and let the soup simmer gently for about 1.5 to 2 hours, or until the meat and vegetables are tender.
5. Skim off any foam or fat that rises to the surface of the soup during cooking.
6. Once the soup is cooked and the meat and vegetables are tender, taste and adjust the seasoning if needed.
7. Remove the bay leaf from the soup before serving.
8. Ladle the hot kjötsúpa into bowls and garnish with chopped fresh parsley.
9. Serve the Icelandic Meat Soup hot, accompanied by slices of crusty bread or Icelandic rye bread.

Enjoy this comforting and nourishing traditional Icelandic dish, packed with the flavors of lamb and hearty vegetables!

Icelandic Lamb Stew

Ingredients:

- 500g lamb meat (such as shoulder or leg), diced
- 2 tablespoons vegetable oil
- 1 onion, finely chopped
- 2 carrots, peeled and diced
- 2 potatoes, peeled and diced
- 1 turnip, peeled and diced
- 1 parsnip, peeled and diced
- 2 celery stalks, chopped
- 2 cloves garlic, minced
- 2 bay leaves
- 1 teaspoon dried thyme
- 1 teaspoon dried rosemary
- 1 liter beef or vegetable broth
- Salt and pepper to taste
- Chopped fresh parsley for garnish

Instructions:

1. Heat the vegetable oil in a large pot or Dutch oven over medium heat. Add the diced lamb meat and brown it on all sides, about 5-7 minutes. Remove the lamb from the pot and set it aside.
2. In the same pot, add the chopped onion and sauté until softened, about 3-4 minutes.
3. Add the minced garlic to the pot and cook for another 1-2 minutes, until fragrant.
4. Return the browned lamb meat to the pot. Add the diced carrots, potatoes, turnip, parsnip, celery, bay leaves, dried thyme, and dried rosemary.
5. Pour in the beef or vegetable broth, enough to cover the ingredients by about 2 inches. Bring the stew to a boil over medium-high heat.
6. Once boiling, reduce the heat to low and let the stew simmer gently, covered, for about 1.5 to 2 hours, or until the lamb and vegetables are tender.
7. Skim off any foam or fat that rises to the surface of the stew during cooking.
8. Taste and adjust the seasoning with salt and pepper as needed.
9. Remove the bay leaves from the stew before serving.
10. Ladle the hot Icelandic lamb stew into bowls and garnish with chopped fresh parsley.

11. Serve the stew hot, accompanied by slices of crusty bread or Icelandic rye bread.

Enjoy this comforting and flavorful Icelandic lamb stew, perfect for a cozy meal at home!

Hangikjöt (Smoked Lamb)

Ingredients:

- 1 kg boneless lamb leg or shoulder, trimmed of excess fat
- 2 tablespoons coarse salt
- 1 tablespoon whole black peppercorns
- 1 tablespoon whole allspice berries
- 1 tablespoon brown sugar
- 2 bay leaves
- Water, as needed
- 1/4 cup liquid smoke (optional, if you don't have access to a smoker)

Instructions:

1. In a large pot, dissolve the coarse salt, whole black peppercorns, whole allspice berries, brown sugar, and bay leaves in enough water to completely submerge the lamb.
2. Place the lamb in the brine mixture, making sure it is fully covered. If necessary, weigh down the lamb with a plate to keep it submerged.
3. Cover the pot and refrigerate for 24-48 hours, allowing the lamb to brine and absorb the flavors.
4. After brining, remove the lamb from the brine and rinse it thoroughly under cold water to remove any excess salt and spices. Pat dry with paper towels.
5. If you have access to a smoker, smoke the lamb according to the manufacturer's instructions until it is cooked through and has absorbed a rich smoky flavor. This typically takes 4-6 hours, depending on the size of the lamb and the temperature of the smoker.
6. If you don't have a smoker, you can achieve a similar flavor by using liquid smoke. Simply brush the liquid smoke over the surface of the lamb and bake it in the oven at 160°C (320°F) for 2-3 hours, or until cooked through and tender.
7. Once cooked, allow the smoked lamb to cool slightly before slicing it thinly.
8. Serve the hangikjöt (smoked lamb) slices warm or cold, accompanied by traditional Icelandic sides such as mashed potatoes, rye bread, pickled red cabbage, and mustard.

Enjoy this delicious and flavorful Icelandic delicacy, perfect for festive occasions and gatherings with family and friends!

Grilled Arctic Char with Lemon-Dill Sauce

Ingredients:

For the Grilled Arctic Char:

- 4 Arctic char fillets
- 2 tablespoons olive oil
- Salt and pepper to taste
- Lemon wedges for serving

For the Lemon-Dill Sauce:

- 1/2 cup mayonnaise
- 2 tablespoons fresh lemon juice
- 1 tablespoon chopped fresh dill
- 1 teaspoon Dijon mustard
- 1 clove garlic, minced
- Salt and pepper to taste

Instructions:

1. Preheat your grill to medium-high heat.
2. Pat the Arctic char fillets dry with paper towels and brush them lightly with olive oil. Season with salt and pepper to taste.
3. Place the Arctic char fillets on the preheated grill, skin side down. Grill for 4-5 minutes, then carefully flip them over using a spatula. Grill for another 4-5 minutes, or until the fish is cooked through and flakes easily with a fork.
4. While the fish is grilling, prepare the lemon-dill sauce. In a small bowl, whisk together the mayonnaise, fresh lemon juice, chopped fresh dill, Dijon mustard, minced garlic, salt, and pepper until smooth and well combined. Adjust seasoning to taste.
5. Once the Arctic char fillets are cooked, remove them from the grill and transfer them to a serving platter.
6. Drizzle the grilled Arctic char fillets with the lemon-dill sauce or serve the sauce on the side.
7. Garnish the dish with additional fresh dill and lemon wedges.

8. Serve the Grilled Arctic Char with Lemon-Dill Sauce immediately, accompanied by your favorite side dishes such as roasted vegetables, steamed rice, or a fresh salad.

Enjoy this delicious and elegant dish, perfect for a special dinner or outdoor barbecue!

Pönnukökur (Icelandic Pancakes) with Jam

Ingredients:

- 1 cup all-purpose flour
- 1 tablespoon sugar
- 1/2 teaspoon baking powder
- 1/4 teaspoon salt
- 2 large eggs
- 1 cup milk
- Butter or oil for cooking
- Jam or your favorite toppings for serving

Instructions:

1. In a large mixing bowl, whisk together the flour, sugar, baking powder, and salt until well combined.
2. In a separate bowl, beat the eggs, then add the milk and whisk until smooth.
3. Gradually pour the wet ingredients into the dry ingredients, stirring constantly, until you have a smooth batter. Let the batter rest for about 10-15 minutes to allow the flour to absorb the liquid.
4. Heat a non-stick skillet or griddle over medium heat. Add a small amount of butter or oil to the skillet and swirl it around to coat the bottom evenly.
5. Pour a small ladleful of batter into the skillet, tilting and swirling the skillet to spread the batter into a thin, even layer.
6. Cook the pancake for 1-2 minutes, or until the edges start to lift and the bottom is golden brown. Use a spatula to flip the pancake and cook for another 1-2 minutes on the other side, until golden brown and cooked through.
7. Transfer the cooked pancake to a plate and cover with a clean kitchen towel to keep warm. Repeat the process with the remaining batter, adding more butter or oil to the skillet as needed.
8. Serve the Pönnukökur hot, with jam or your favorite toppings such as whipped cream, fresh berries, or maple syrup.

Enjoy these delicious Icelandic pancakes as a breakfast treat or a sweet snack!

Kjúklingur í Fati (Chicken in Cream Sauce)

Ingredients:

- 4 boneless, skinless chicken breasts
- Salt and pepper to taste
- 2 tablespoons olive oil
- 1 onion, finely chopped
- 2 cloves garlic, minced
- 1 cup chicken broth
- 1 cup heavy cream
- 2 tablespoons Dijon mustard
- 1 tablespoon chopped fresh parsley
- 1 tablespoon chopped fresh thyme (or 1 teaspoon dried thyme)
- 1 tablespoon chopped fresh rosemary (or 1 teaspoon dried rosemary)

Instructions:

1. Season the chicken breasts with salt and pepper to taste.
2. In a large skillet, heat the olive oil over medium-high heat. Add the chicken breasts and cook until browned on both sides, about 4-5 minutes per side. Remove the chicken from the skillet and set aside.
3. In the same skillet, add the chopped onion and cook until softened, about 3-4 minutes. Add the minced garlic and cook for another 1-2 minutes, until fragrant.
4. Pour in the chicken broth and bring to a simmer, scraping up any browned bits from the bottom of the skillet.
5. Reduce the heat to medium-low and stir in the heavy cream, Dijon mustard, chopped fresh parsley, thyme, and rosemary. Simmer for 5-7 minutes, until the sauce has thickened slightly.
6. Return the browned chicken breasts to the skillet, nestling them into the sauce. Spoon some of the sauce over the chicken.
7. Cover the skillet and simmer gently for 10-12 minutes, or until the chicken is cooked through and no longer pink in the center, and the sauce has thickened further.
8. Taste the sauce and adjust seasoning with salt and pepper if needed.
9. Serve the Chicken in Cream Sauce hot, garnished with additional chopped fresh herbs if desired.
10. Enjoy this delicious and comforting dish with mashed potatoes, rice, or pasta, and your favorite vegetables on the side.

This Chicken in Cream Sauce recipe is sure to become a family favorite!

Plokkfiskur (Fish and Potato Mash)

Ingredients:

- 500g white fish fillets (such as cod, haddock, or pollock), cut into bite-sized pieces
- 500g potatoes, peeled and diced into small cubes
- 1 onion, finely chopped
- 2 tablespoons butter
- 2 tablespoons all-purpose flour
- 2 cups milk
- Salt and pepper to taste
- Chopped fresh parsley for garnish

Instructions:

1. Place the diced potatoes in a pot of salted water. Bring to a boil and cook until the potatoes are fork-tender, about 10-15 minutes. Drain and set aside.
2. In a large skillet or saucepan, melt the butter over medium heat. Add the chopped onion and sauté until softened and translucent, about 5 minutes.
3. Sprinkle the flour over the onions and butter, stirring to combine. Cook for another 1-2 minutes to cook off the raw flour taste.
4. Gradually pour in the milk, stirring constantly, until the mixture thickens and becomes smooth and creamy, about 5 minutes.
5. Add the cooked diced potatoes to the skillet with the creamy sauce. Mash the potatoes with a fork or potato masher until smooth and well combined with the sauce.
6. Season the mixture with salt and pepper to taste.
7. Gently fold the bite-sized fish fillet pieces into the creamy potato mixture, being careful not to break up the fish too much.
8. Continue to cook over low heat for another 5-7 minutes, or until the fish is cooked through and flakes easily with a fork.
9. Taste and adjust seasoning if needed.
10. Serve the Plokkfiskur hot, garnished with chopped fresh parsley.

Enjoy this comforting and flavorful Icelandic Fish and Potato Mash, perfect for a cozy meal at home!

Lamb Shank Slow Cooked in Red Wine

Ingredients:

- 4 lamb shanks
- Salt and pepper to taste
- 2 tablespoons olive oil
- 1 onion, finely chopped
- 2 carrots, peeled and diced
- 2 celery stalks, diced
- 4 cloves garlic, minced
- 2 cups red wine (such as Merlot or Cabernet Sauvignon)
- 1 cup beef or vegetable broth
- 2 bay leaves
- 2 sprigs fresh rosemary
- 2 sprigs fresh thyme
- 1 tablespoon tomato paste
- Chopped fresh parsley for garnish (optional)

Instructions:

1. Season the lamb shanks generously with salt and pepper.
2. In a large skillet or Dutch oven, heat the olive oil over medium-high heat. Add the lamb shanks and sear them on all sides until browned, about 4-5 minutes per side. Remove the lamb shanks from the skillet and set aside.
3. In the same skillet, add the chopped onion, diced carrots, and diced celery. Cook, stirring occasionally, until the vegetables are softened, about 5-6 minutes.
4. Add the minced garlic to the skillet and cook for another 1-2 minutes, until fragrant.
5. Pour in the red wine and beef or vegetable broth, stirring to deglaze the bottom of the skillet and scrape up any browned bits.
6. Stir in the tomato paste until well combined.
7. Return the lamb shanks to the skillet, nestling them into the liquid. Add the bay leaves, fresh rosemary, and fresh thyme sprigs.
8. Cover the skillet or Dutch oven and cook the lamb shanks over low heat for 4-6 hours, or until the meat is tender and falling off the bone. Alternatively, you can transfer everything to a slow cooker and cook on low for 6-8 hours.

9. Once the lamb shanks are cooked, remove them from the skillet and transfer to a serving platter.
10. Skim off any excess fat from the cooking liquid, then strain the liquid through a fine mesh sieve into a saucepan. Bring the liquid to a simmer over medium heat and cook until reduced and slightly thickened.
11. Taste the sauce and adjust seasoning if needed.
12. Serve the slow-cooked lamb shanks drizzled with the reduced sauce, and garnish with chopped fresh parsley if desired.

Enjoy this delicious and comforting dish of slow-cooked lamb shanks in red wine, perfect for a special occasion or a cozy dinner at home!

Pan-Fried Cod with Lemon Butter Sauce

Ingredients:

For the Pan-Fried Cod:

- 4 cod fillets (about 150-200g each), skin removed
- Salt and pepper to taste
- 2 tablespoons all-purpose flour
- 2 tablespoons olive oil
- 2 tablespoons butter

For the Lemon Butter Sauce:

- 1/4 cup unsalted butter
- 2 cloves garlic, minced
- Zest of 1 lemon
- Juice of 1 lemon
- 2 tablespoons chopped fresh parsley
- Salt and pepper to taste

Instructions:

1. Pat the cod fillets dry with paper towels and season them with salt and pepper to taste. Lightly dust both sides of the cod fillets with flour, shaking off any excess.
2. Heat the olive oil and butter in a large skillet over medium-high heat. Once the butter has melted and the skillet is hot, add the cod fillets to the skillet.
3. Cook the cod fillets for 3-4 minutes on each side, or until they are golden brown and cooked through. The internal temperature of the cod should reach 145°F (63°C) when properly cooked.
4. While the cod is cooking, prepare the lemon butter sauce. In a small saucepan, melt the butter over medium heat. Add the minced garlic and cook for 1-2 minutes, until fragrant.
5. Stir in the lemon zest and lemon juice, then add the chopped fresh parsley. Season the sauce with salt and pepper to taste.
6. Once the cod fillets are cooked, transfer them to a serving platter.
7. Pour the lemon butter sauce over the pan-fried cod fillets.
8. Garnish with additional chopped parsley and lemon wedges if desired.

9. Serve the pan-fried cod with lemon butter sauce immediately, accompanied by your favorite side dishes such as steamed vegetables, rice, or mashed potatoes.

Enjoy this delicious and elegant dish of pan-fried cod with lemon butter sauce, perfect for a special dinner or any occasion!

Fisherman's Lamb Stew with Root Vegetables

Ingredients:

- 1.5 kg lamb stew meat, cut into bite-sized pieces
- Salt and pepper to taste
- 2 tablespoons olive oil
- 1 onion, diced
- 2 carrots, peeled and diced
- 2 parsnips, peeled and diced
- 2 celery stalks, diced
- 4 cloves garlic, minced
- 2 tablespoons tomato paste
- 1 tablespoon all-purpose flour
- 1 cup red wine
- 4 cups beef or vegetable broth
- 2 bay leaves
- 2 sprigs fresh thyme
- 2 sprigs fresh rosemary
- 2 potatoes, peeled and diced
- 2 turnips, peeled and diced
- Chopped fresh parsley for garnish

Instructions:

1. Season the lamb stew meat with salt and pepper to taste.
2. Heat the olive oil in a large Dutch oven or heavy-bottomed pot over medium-high heat. Add the lamb stew meat and cook until browned on all sides, about 6-8 minutes. Remove the lamb from the pot and set aside.
3. In the same pot, add the diced onion, carrots, parsnips, and celery. Cook, stirring occasionally, until the vegetables are softened, about 5-6 minutes.
4. Add the minced garlic to the pot and cook for another 1-2 minutes, until fragrant.
5. Stir in the tomato paste and flour, and cook for 1-2 minutes to cook off the raw flavor of the flour.
6. Pour in the red wine and deglaze the bottom of the pot, scraping up any browned bits with a wooden spoon.
7. Return the browned lamb stew meat to the pot. Pour in the beef or vegetable broth, and add the bay leaves, fresh thyme, and fresh rosemary.

8. Bring the stew to a simmer, then reduce the heat to low. Cover the pot and let the stew simmer gently for 1.5 to 2 hours, or until the lamb is tender.
9. Once the lamb is tender, add the diced potatoes and turnips to the pot. Continue to simmer the stew, uncovered, for another 20-30 minutes, or until the vegetables are cooked through and the stew has thickened slightly.
10. Taste the stew and adjust seasoning with salt and pepper if needed.
11. Remove the bay leaves, thyme sprigs, and rosemary sprigs from the stew before serving.
12. Ladle the Fisherman's lamb stew into bowls and garnish with chopped fresh parsley.

Enjoy this hearty and comforting Fisherman's lamb stew with root vegetables, perfect for a cozy meal on a chilly day!

Icelandic Fish Pie

Ingredients:

For the Fish Filling:

- 500g white fish fillets (such as cod, haddock, or pollock), cut into bite-sized pieces
- 1 onion, finely chopped
- 2 carrots, peeled and diced
- 2 celery stalks, diced
- 2 tablespoons butter
- 2 tablespoons all-purpose flour
- 1 cup milk
- 1 cup fish or vegetable broth
- 2 tablespoons chopped fresh parsley
- Salt and pepper to taste

For the Mashed Potato Topping:

- 4 large potatoes, peeled and diced
- 4 tablespoons butter
- 1/2 cup milk
- Salt and pepper to taste

Instructions:

1. Preheat your oven to 180°C (350°F). Grease a baking dish with butter or cooking spray and set aside.
2. To make the fish filling, melt the butter in a large skillet over medium heat. Add the chopped onion, diced carrots, and diced celery. Cook, stirring occasionally, until the vegetables are softened, about 5-6 minutes.
3. Sprinkle the flour over the vegetables and stir to coat evenly. Cook for another 1-2 minutes to cook off the raw flour taste.
4. Gradually pour in the milk and fish or vegetable broth, stirring constantly, until the mixture thickens and becomes smooth and creamy.

5. Add the chopped fresh parsley to the sauce, then gently fold in the bite-sized fish fillet pieces. Season with salt and pepper to taste.
6. Pour the fish filling into the prepared baking dish, spreading it out evenly.
7. To make the mashed potato topping, place the diced potatoes in a large pot of salted water. Bring to a boil and cook until the potatoes are fork-tender, about 10-15 minutes. Drain the potatoes and return them to the pot.
8. Add the butter and milk to the pot with the cooked potatoes. Mash the potatoes with a potato masher until smooth and creamy. Season with salt and pepper to taste.
9. Spread the mashed potato topping over the fish filling in the baking dish, smoothing it out with a spatula.
10. Bake the Icelandic fish pie in the preheated oven for 25-30 minutes, or until the mashed potato topping is golden brown and the filling is bubbling.
11. Remove the fish pie from the oven and let it cool for a few minutes before serving.
12. Serve the Icelandic fish pie hot, garnished with additional chopped fresh parsley if desired.

Enjoy this comforting and flavorful dish of Icelandic fish pie, perfect for a cozy meal with family and friends!

Baked Arctic Char with Herb Crust

Ingredients:

- 4 Arctic char fillets
- Salt and pepper to taste
- 2 tablespoons olive oil

For the Herb Crust:

- 1/2 cup breadcrumbs
- 2 tablespoons chopped fresh parsley
- 1 tablespoon chopped fresh dill
- 1 tablespoon chopped fresh chives
- 1 tablespoon chopped fresh thyme (or 1 teaspoon dried thyme)
- 1 tablespoon chopped fresh rosemary (or 1 teaspoon dried rosemary)
- 2 tablespoons melted butter
- Zest of 1 lemon
- Salt and pepper to taste

Instructions:

1. Preheat your oven to 200°C (400°F). Grease a baking dish with olive oil or cooking spray and set aside.
2. Season the Arctic char fillets with salt and pepper to taste. Place them in the prepared baking dish.
3. In a small bowl, combine the breadcrumbs, chopped fresh herbs (parsley, dill, chives, thyme, and rosemary), melted butter, lemon zest, salt, and pepper. Mix until well combined.
4. Press the herb crust mixture onto the top of each Arctic char fillet, covering them evenly.
5. Drizzle the olive oil over the herb-crusted Arctic char fillets.
6. Bake the Arctic char in the preheated oven for 12-15 minutes, or until the fish is cooked through and flakes easily with a fork.
7. Once cooked, remove the Arctic char from the oven and let it rest for a few minutes before serving.
8. Serve the Baked Arctic Char with Herb Crust hot, garnished with additional chopped fresh herbs and lemon wedges if desired.

Enjoy this flavorful and elegant dish of Baked Arctic Char with Herb Crust, perfect for a special occasion or a romantic dinner!

Lamb Chops with Rosemary and Garlic

Ingredients:

- 4 lamb loin chops
- Salt and pepper to taste
- 2 tablespoons olive oil
- 4 cloves garlic, minced
- 2 tablespoons fresh rosemary leaves, chopped (or 2 teaspoons dried rosemary)

Instructions:

1. Preheat your oven to 200°C (400°F).
2. Season the lamb loin chops generously with salt and pepper on both sides.
3. In a small bowl, combine the minced garlic and chopped rosemary.
4. Rub the garlic and rosemary mixture onto both sides of each lamb chop, pressing it gently to adhere.
5. Heat the olive oil in a large oven-safe skillet over medium-high heat.
6. Once the skillet is hot, add the lamb chops and sear them for 2-3 minutes on each side, until browned.
7. Transfer the skillet to the preheated oven and roast the lamb chops for about 10-12 minutes, or until they reach your desired level of doneness. For medium-rare, the internal temperature should reach 60-65°C (140-150°F).
8. Once cooked to your liking, remove the lamb chops from the oven and let them rest for a few minutes before serving.
9. Serve the lamb chops hot, garnished with additional fresh rosemary if desired.

Enjoy these delicious and aromatic lamb chops with rosemary and garlic as a main course for a special dinner! They pair wonderfully with roasted vegetables, mashed potatoes, or a fresh green salad.

Grilled Langoustines with Garlic Butter

Ingredients:

- 12 langoustines (also known as Dublin Bay prawns or Norway lobsters), cleaned and deveined
- Salt and pepper to taste
- 4 tablespoons unsalted butter, softened
- 4 cloves garlic, minced
- 2 tablespoons chopped fresh parsley
- Lemon wedges, for serving

Instructions:

1. Preheat your grill to medium-high heat.
2. Season the langoustines with salt and pepper to taste.
3. In a small bowl, mix together the softened butter, minced garlic, and chopped fresh parsley until well combined.
4. Place the langoustines on the preheated grill, shell side down. Grill for about 2-3 minutes, until the shells turn pink and the meat is opaque and slightly charred.
5. Flip the langoustines over and grill for another 2-3 minutes on the other side, until the meat is fully cooked through.
6. Once the langoustines are cooked, remove them from the grill and transfer them to a serving platter.
7. While the langoustines are still hot, spoon the garlic butter mixture over them, allowing it to melt and coat the langoustines.
8. Serve the grilled langoustines with garlic butter immediately, accompanied by lemon wedges for squeezing over the top.
9. Enjoy the succulent and flavorful grilled langoustines as a delightful appetizer or main course!

This dish is perfect for entertaining guests or as a special treat for yourself. The combination of tender langoustine meat and rich garlic butter is sure to impress!

Icelandic Fish Stew with Vegetables

Ingredients:

- 500g white fish fillets (such as cod, haddock, or pollock), cut into bite-sized pieces
- 1 onion, chopped
- 2 carrots, peeled and diced
- 2 celery stalks, diced
- 2 potatoes, peeled and diced
- 2 tablespoons butter
- 4 cups fish or vegetable broth
- 1 cup milk
- 1/4 cup all-purpose flour
- 2 bay leaves
- Salt and pepper to taste
- Chopped fresh parsley for garnish

Instructions:

1. In a large pot or Dutch oven, melt the butter over medium heat. Add the chopped onion, diced carrots, diced celery, and diced potatoes. Cook, stirring occasionally, until the vegetables are softened, about 5-6 minutes.
2. Sprinkle the flour over the vegetables and stir to coat evenly. Cook for another 1-2 minutes to cook off the raw flour taste.
3. Gradually pour in the fish or vegetable broth, stirring constantly, until the mixture thickens and becomes smooth and creamy.
4. Stir in the milk and add the bay leaves. Bring the stew to a simmer, then reduce the heat to low. Cover the pot and let the stew simmer gently for about 15-20 minutes, or until the vegetables are tender.
5. Once the vegetables are cooked, add the bite-sized fish fillet pieces to the pot. Continue to simmer the stew for another 5-7 minutes, or until the fish is cooked through and flakes easily with a fork.
6. Taste the stew and season with salt and pepper to taste.
7. Remove the bay leaves from the stew before serving.
8. Ladle the Icelandic fish stew with vegetables into bowls and garnish with chopped fresh parsley.
9. Serve the fish stew hot, accompanied by crusty bread or crackers.

Enjoy this comforting and flavorful Icelandic fish stew with vegetables, perfect for a cozy meal at home!

Braised Lamb Shanks with Redcurrant Sauce

Ingredients:

- 4 lamb shanks
- Salt and pepper to taste
- 2 tablespoons olive oil
- 1 onion, finely chopped
- 2 carrots, peeled and diced
- 2 celery stalks, diced
- 4 cloves garlic, minced
- 2 cups beef or vegetable broth
- 1 cup red wine
- 1/4 cup redcurrant jelly
- 2 tablespoons tomato paste
- 2 bay leaves
- 2 sprigs fresh rosemary
- Chopped fresh parsley for garnish

Instructions:

1. Preheat your oven to 160°C (325°F).
2. Season the lamb shanks generously with salt and pepper.
3. Heat the olive oil in a large Dutch oven or heavy-bottomed pot over medium-high heat. Add the lamb shanks and sear them on all sides until browned, about 6-8 minutes. Remove the lamb shanks from the pot and set aside.
4. In the same pot, add the chopped onion, diced carrots, and diced celery. Cook, stirring occasionally, until the vegetables are softened, about 5-6 minutes.
5. Add the minced garlic to the pot and cook for another 1-2 minutes, until fragrant.
6. Pour in the beef or vegetable broth and red wine, stirring to deglaze the bottom of the pot and scrape up any browned bits.
7. Stir in the redcurrant jelly and tomato paste until well combined.
8. Return the browned lamb shanks to the pot. Add the bay leaves and fresh rosemary sprigs.
9. Cover the pot and transfer it to the preheated oven. Braise the lamb shanks for 2-2.5 hours, or until the meat is tender and falling off the bone.
10. Once the lamb shanks are cooked, remove them from the pot and transfer them to a serving platter.

11. Strain the cooking liquid through a fine mesh sieve into a saucepan. Bring the liquid to a simmer over medium heat and cook until reduced and slightly thickened.
12. Taste the sauce and adjust seasoning if needed.
13. Serve the braised lamb shanks with redcurrant sauce hot, garnished with chopped fresh parsley.

Enjoy this delicious and elegant dish of braised lamb shanks with redcurrant sauce, perfect for a special occasion or a cozy dinner at home!

Pan-Seared Cod with Tomato and Olive Tapenade

Ingredients:

For the Tomato and Olive Tapenade:

- 1 cup cherry tomatoes, halved
- 1/2 cup pitted Kalamata olives, chopped
- 2 tablespoons capers, drained and chopped
- 2 cloves garlic, minced
- 2 tablespoons chopped fresh basil
- 1 tablespoon chopped fresh parsley
- 1 tablespoon lemon juice
- 2 tablespoons extra virgin olive oil
- Salt and pepper to taste

For the Pan-Seared Cod:

- 4 cod fillets
- Salt and pepper to taste
- 2 tablespoons olive oil
- Lemon wedges, for serving
- Chopped fresh parsley, for garnish

Instructions:

1. In a medium bowl, combine the halved cherry tomatoes, chopped Kalamata olives, chopped capers, minced garlic, chopped fresh basil, chopped fresh parsley, lemon juice, and extra virgin olive oil. Season with salt and pepper to taste. Mix well to combine and set aside.
2. Season the cod fillets generously with salt and pepper on both sides.
3. Heat the olive oil in a large skillet over medium-high heat.
4. Once the skillet is hot, add the cod fillets to the skillet, skin side down. Cook for about 4-5 minutes, until the skin is golden and crispy.
5. Carefully flip the cod fillets over and continue to cook for another 3-4 minutes, or until the fish is cooked through and flakes easily with a fork.
6. Once the cod fillets are cooked, transfer them to serving plates.
7. Spoon the tomato and olive tapenade over the top of each cod fillet.

8. Garnish the cod fillets with chopped fresh parsley and serve immediately with lemon wedges on the side.
9. Enjoy this delicious and flavorful pan-seared cod with tomato and olive tapenade as a main course for a light and satisfying meal!

This dish pairs well with steamed vegetables, roasted potatoes, or a simple green salad.

Icelandic Meatballs with Mushroom Gravy

Ingredients:

For the Meatballs:

- 500g ground beef or a mix of ground beef and pork
- 1/2 cup breadcrumbs
- 1/4 cup milk
- 1 onion, finely chopped
- 2 cloves garlic, minced
- 1 egg
- 1 tablespoon chopped fresh parsley
- 1 teaspoon salt
- 1/2 teaspoon black pepper
- 1/4 teaspoon ground nutmeg

For the Mushroom Gravy:

- 2 tablespoons butter
- 250g mushrooms, sliced
- 1 onion, finely chopped
- 2 cloves garlic, minced
- 2 tablespoons all-purpose flour
- 2 cups beef or vegetable broth
- 1/2 cup heavy cream
- Salt and pepper to taste
- Chopped fresh parsley for garnish

Instructions:

1. Preheat your oven to 180°C (350°F). Grease a baking sheet or line it with parchment paper.
2. In a small bowl, mix together the breadcrumbs and milk. Let it sit for a few minutes until the breadcrumbs absorb the milk.
3. In a large mixing bowl, combine the ground beef (or beef and pork mix), soaked breadcrumbs, chopped onion, minced garlic, egg, chopped parsley, salt, pepper, and ground nutmeg. Mix until well combined.

4. Shape the mixture into meatballs, about 1-1.5 inches in diameter, and place them on the prepared baking sheet.
5. Bake the meatballs in the preheated oven for 20-25 minutes, or until they are cooked through and browned on the outside.
6. While the meatballs are baking, prepare the mushroom gravy. In a large skillet, melt the butter over medium heat. Add the sliced mushrooms and chopped onion. Cook, stirring occasionally, until the mushrooms are tender and golden brown, and the onions are translucent, about 6-8 minutes.
7. Add the minced garlic to the skillet and cook for another 1-2 minutes, until fragrant.
8. Sprinkle the flour over the mushrooms and onions, and stir to coat evenly. Cook for 1-2 minutes to cook off the raw flour taste.
9. Gradually pour in the beef or vegetable broth, stirring constantly, until the mixture thickens and becomes smooth.
10. Stir in the heavy cream and continue to cook for another 2-3 minutes, until the gravy is heated through and thickened to your desired consistency. Season with salt and pepper to taste.
11. Once the meatballs are cooked, transfer them to a serving platter. Pour the mushroom gravy over the meatballs.
12. Garnish with chopped fresh parsley and serve the Icelandic meatballs with mushroom gravy hot, accompanied by mashed potatoes, rice, or pasta.

Enjoy this comforting and delicious dish of Icelandic meatballs with mushroom gravy!

Baked Salmon with Honey-Dijon Glaze

Ingredients:

- 4 salmon fillets (about 150-200g each), skin-on or skinless
- Salt and pepper to taste
- 2 tablespoons honey
- 2 tablespoons Dijon mustard
- 1 tablespoon soy sauce (or tamari for gluten-free)
- 1 tablespoon olive oil
- 2 cloves garlic, minced
- 1 tablespoon fresh lemon juice
- Chopped fresh parsley for garnish (optional)
- Lemon wedges, for serving

Instructions:

1. Preheat your oven to 200°C (400°F). Line a baking sheet with parchment paper or lightly grease it with cooking spray.
2. Season the salmon fillets with salt and pepper to taste, and place them on the prepared baking sheet.
3. In a small bowl, whisk together the honey, Dijon mustard, soy sauce, olive oil, minced garlic, and fresh lemon juice until well combined.
4. Spoon the honey-Dijon glaze over the salmon fillets, spreading it evenly to coat each piece.
5. Bake the salmon in the preheated oven for 12-15 minutes, or until the salmon is cooked through and flakes easily with a fork. The cooking time will depend on the thickness of your salmon fillets.
6. Once the salmon is cooked, remove it from the oven and let it rest for a few minutes before serving.
7. Garnish the baked salmon with chopped fresh parsley if desired, and serve with lemon wedges on the side.
8. Enjoy this delicious baked salmon with honey-Dijon glaze as a main course, paired with your favorite side dishes such as roasted vegetables, rice, or salad.

This dish is quick, easy, and packed with flavor, making it perfect for a weeknight dinner or a special occasion!

Icelandic Lamb Chops with Mint Sauce

Ingredients:

For the Lamb Chops:

- 8 lamb loin chops
- Salt and pepper to taste
- 2 tablespoons olive oil

For the Mint Sauce:

- 1/2 cup fresh mint leaves, finely chopped
- 2 tablespoons white wine vinegar
- 1 tablespoon sugar
- 2 tablespoons boiling water
- Salt and pepper to taste

Instructions:

1. Preheat your grill or grill pan to medium-high heat.
2. Season the lamb chops with salt and pepper to taste.
3. Drizzle the olive oil over the lamb chops, rubbing it into both sides of each chop.
4. Place the lamb chops on the preheated grill or grill pan and cook for about 3-4 minutes on each side, or until they reach your desired level of doneness. For medium-rare, the internal temperature should reach 60-65°C (140-150°F).
5. While the lamb chops are cooking, prepare the mint sauce. In a small bowl, combine the finely chopped mint leaves, white wine vinegar, sugar, and boiling water. Stir until the sugar is dissolved. Season with salt and pepper to taste.
6. Once the lamb chops are cooked to your liking, remove them from the grill and transfer them to a serving platter.
7. Serve the grilled Icelandic lamb chops hot, accompanied by the mint sauce on the side.
8. Enjoy this delicious and flavorful dish of Icelandic lamb chops with mint sauce, perfect for a special occasion or a festive dinner!

These lamb chops pair well with roasted vegetables, mashed potatoes, or a fresh green salad for a complete and satisfying meal.

Slow Cooked Lamb Shoulder with Root Vegetables

Ingredients:

- 1 lamb shoulder (about 2-3 kg), bone-in or boneless
- Salt and pepper to taste
- 2 tablespoons olive oil
- 4 cloves garlic, minced
- 2 onions, sliced
- 4 carrots, peeled and cut into chunks
- 4 parsnips, peeled and cut into chunks
- 2 large potatoes, peeled and cut into chunks
- 2 cups beef or vegetable broth
- 1 cup red wine (optional)
- 2 bay leaves
- 2 sprigs fresh rosemary
- 2 sprigs fresh thyme

Instructions:

1. Preheat your oven to 160°C (325°F).
2. Season the lamb shoulder generously with salt and pepper on all sides.
3. Heat the olive oil in a large Dutch oven or heavy-bottomed pot over medium-high heat. Add the lamb shoulder to the pot and sear it on all sides until browned, about 4-5 minutes per side. Remove the lamb shoulder from the pot and set it aside.
4. In the same pot, add the minced garlic and sliced onions. Cook, stirring occasionally, until the onions are softened and translucent, about 5-6 minutes.
5. Add the carrots, parsnips, and potatoes to the pot, and cook for another 3-4 minutes, stirring occasionally.
6. Place the seared lamb shoulder on top of the vegetables in the pot.
7. Pour the beef or vegetable broth and red wine (if using) over the lamb shoulder and vegetables. Add the bay leaves, fresh rosemary, and fresh thyme to the pot.
8. Cover the pot with a lid and transfer it to the preheated oven.
9. Slow-cook the lamb shoulder in the oven for 3-4 hours, or until the meat is tender and falling off the bone.

10. Once the lamb shoulder is cooked, remove it from the pot and transfer it to a serving platter. Use a slotted spoon to transfer the vegetables to the platter as well.
11. Serve the slow-cooked lamb shoulder with root vegetables hot, accompanied by the cooking juices spooned over the top.
12. Enjoy this comforting and flavorful dish of slow-cooked lamb shoulder with root vegetables, perfect for a comforting family meal or a special occasion!

Feel free to adjust the seasoning and add additional herbs or spices to suit your taste preferences.

Pan-Fried Haddock with Caper Cream Sauce

Ingredients:

For the Pan-Fried Haddock:

- 4 haddock fillets (about 150-200g each)
- Salt and pepper to taste
- 2 tablespoons olive oil
- 2 tablespoons butter

For the Caper Cream Sauce:

- 2 tablespoons butter
- 2 tablespoons all-purpose flour
- 1 cup fish or vegetable broth
- 1/2 cup heavy cream
- 2 tablespoons capers, drained
- 1 tablespoon lemon juice
- Salt and pepper to taste
- Chopped fresh parsley for garnish

Instructions:

1. Season the haddock fillets generously with salt and pepper on both sides.
2. In a large skillet, heat the olive oil and butter over medium-high heat.
3. Once the skillet is hot, add the haddock fillets to the pan. Cook for about 3-4 minutes on each side, or until the fish is cooked through and flakes easily with a fork. The cooking time will depend on the thickness of the fillets.
4. While the haddock is cooking, prepare the caper cream sauce. In a separate saucepan, melt the butter over medium heat. Add the flour and whisk continuously for 1-2 minutes to create a roux.
5. Gradually pour in the fish or vegetable broth, whisking constantly to prevent lumps from forming. Cook for 2-3 minutes, or until the sauce thickens.
6. Stir in the heavy cream, capers, and lemon juice. Continue to cook for another 2-3 minutes, until the sauce is smooth and heated through. Season with salt and pepper to taste.
7. Once the haddock fillets are cooked, transfer them to serving plates.
8. Spoon the caper cream sauce over the haddock fillets.

9. Garnish with chopped fresh parsley and serve immediately.

Enjoy this delicious and elegant dish of pan-fried haddock with caper cream sauce, perfect for a special dinner or a romantic meal at home!

Grilled Prawns with Chili-Lime Butter

Ingredients:

For the Pan-Fried Haddock:

- 4 haddock fillets (about 150-200g each)
- Salt and pepper to taste
- 2 tablespoons olive oil
- 2 tablespoons butter

For the Caper Cream Sauce:

- 2 tablespoons butter
- 2 tablespoons all-purpose flour
- 1 cup fish or vegetable broth
- 1/2 cup heavy cream
- 2 tablespoons capers, drained
- 1 tablespoon lemon juice
- Salt and pepper to taste
- Chopped fresh parsley for garnish

Instructions:

1. Season the haddock fillets generously with salt and pepper on both sides.
2. In a large skillet, heat the olive oil and butter over medium-high heat.
3. Once the skillet is hot, add the haddock fillets to the pan. Cook for about 3-4 minutes on each side, or until the fish is cooked through and flakes easily with a fork. The cooking time will depend on the thickness of the fillets.
4. While the haddock is cooking, prepare the caper cream sauce. In a separate saucepan, melt the butter over medium heat. Add the flour and whisk continuously for 1-2 minutes to create a roux.
5. Gradually pour in the fish or vegetable broth, whisking constantly to prevent lumps from forming. Cook for 2-3 minutes, or until the sauce thickens.
6. Stir in the heavy cream, capers, and lemon juice. Continue to cook for another 2-3 minutes, until the sauce is smooth and heated through. Season with salt and pepper to taste.

7. Once the haddock fillets are cooked, transfer them to serving plates.
8. Spoon the caper cream sauce over the haddock fillets.
9. Garnish with chopped fresh parsley and serve immediately.

Enjoy this delicious and elegant dish of pan-fried haddock with caper cream sauce, perfect for a special dinner or a romantic meal at home!

Fish and Vegetable Stir-Fry

Ingredients:

- 400g firm white fish fillets (such as cod, haddock, or tilapia), cut into bite-sized pieces
- Salt and pepper to taste
- 2 tablespoons soy sauce
- 1 tablespoon rice vinegar
- 1 tablespoon honey or brown sugar
- 2 cloves garlic, minced
- 1 tablespoon grated fresh ginger
- 2 tablespoons vegetable oil, divided
- 1 onion, thinly sliced
- 1 bell pepper, thinly sliced
- 1 carrot, julienned
- 1 cup broccoli florets
- 1 cup snow peas, trimmed
- 1 cup sliced mushrooms
- Cooked rice or noodles, for serving
- Chopped green onions and sesame seeds for garnish (optional)

Instructions:

1. Season the fish fillets with salt and pepper to taste. In a small bowl, whisk together the soy sauce, rice vinegar, honey or brown sugar, minced garlic, and grated ginger. Pour half of the sauce over the fish fillets and let them marinate for about 15-20 minutes.
2. Heat 1 tablespoon of vegetable oil in a large skillet or wok over medium-high heat. Add the marinated fish fillets to the skillet and cook for 2-3 minutes on each side, or until the fish is cooked through and flakes easily with a fork. Remove the fish from the skillet and set it aside.
3. In the same skillet, heat the remaining tablespoon of vegetable oil. Add the sliced onion, bell pepper, carrot, broccoli florets, snow peas, and mushrooms to the skillet. Stir-fry for 3-4 minutes, or until the vegetables are tender-crisp.
4. Return the cooked fish to the skillet with the vegetables. Pour the remaining sauce over the fish and vegetables, and toss everything together until well coated and heated through.

5. Serve the fish and vegetable stir-fry hot over cooked rice or noodles.
6. Garnish with chopped green onions and sesame seeds, if desired.

Enjoy this delicious and nutritious fish and vegetable stir-fry as a quick and satisfying meal! You can customize the vegetables based on your preferences or what you have on hand.

Lamb Shoulder Roast with Juniper Berry Sauce

Ingredients:

For the Lamb Shoulder Roast:

- 1 bone-in lamb shoulder roast (about 2-3 kg)
- Salt and pepper to taste
- 2 tablespoons olive oil
- 4 cloves garlic, minced
- 2 tablespoons fresh rosemary leaves, chopped
- 2 tablespoons fresh thyme leaves, chopped
- 1 lemon, zest and juice

For the Juniper Berry Sauce:

- 2 tablespoons butter
- 1 onion, finely chopped
- 2 cloves garlic, minced
- 1 cup beef or vegetable broth
- 1/2 cup red wine
- 1 tablespoon juniper berries, crushed
- 1 tablespoon all-purpose flour
- Salt and pepper to taste

Instructions:

1. Preheat your oven to 160°C (325°F).
2. Season the lamb shoulder roast generously with salt and pepper on all sides.
3. In a small bowl, mix together the olive oil, minced garlic, chopped rosemary, chopped thyme, lemon zest, and lemon juice.
4. Rub the herb mixture all over the lamb shoulder roast, coating it evenly.
5. Place the seasoned lamb shoulder roast in a roasting pan or baking dish.
6. Roast the lamb shoulder in the preheated oven for 3-4 hours, or until the meat is tender and falls off the bone.
7. While the lamb is roasting, prepare the juniper berry sauce. In a saucepan, melt the butter over medium heat. Add the chopped onion and minced garlic, and cook until softened, about 5-6 minutes.
8. Stir in the crushed juniper berries and cook for another 1-2 minutes.

9. Sprinkle the flour over the onion and juniper berry mixture, and stir to combine. Cook for 1-2 minutes to cook off the raw flour taste.
10. Gradually pour in the beef or vegetable broth and red wine, stirring constantly to prevent lumps from forming.
11. Bring the sauce to a simmer and cook for 5-10 minutes, or until thickened to your desired consistency. Season with salt and pepper to taste.
12. Once the lamb shoulder roast is cooked, remove it from the oven and let it rest for a few minutes before carving.
13. Serve the sliced lamb shoulder roast with the juniper berry sauce spooned over the top.
14. Enjoy this delicious and flavorful lamb shoulder roast with juniper berry sauce as a centerpiece for your holiday or special occasion dinner!

This dish pairs well with roasted vegetables, mashed potatoes, or a fresh green salad.

Baked Cod with Herbed Crumb Topping

Ingredients:

- 4 cod fillets (about 150-200g each)
- Salt and pepper to taste
- 2 tablespoons olive oil

For the Herbed Crumb Topping:

- 1 cup breadcrumbs (fresh or dried)
- 2 tablespoons melted butter
- 2 cloves garlic, minced
- 1 tablespoon chopped fresh parsley
- 1 tablespoon chopped fresh dill (or 1 teaspoon dried dill)
- 1 teaspoon lemon zest
- Salt and pepper to taste

Instructions:

1. Preheat your oven to 200°C (400°F). Lightly grease a baking dish with olive oil or cooking spray.
2. Pat the cod fillets dry with paper towels and place them in the prepared baking dish. Season both sides of the fillets with salt and pepper to taste.
3. In a small bowl, combine the breadcrumbs, melted butter, minced garlic, chopped fresh parsley, chopped fresh dill, lemon zest, salt, and pepper. Mix well until the breadcrumbs are evenly coated with the butter and herbs.
4. Spoon the herbed crumb topping evenly over the top of each cod fillet, pressing it lightly to adhere.
5. Drizzle the olive oil over the top of the crumb topping.
6. Bake the cod fillets in the preheated oven for 12-15 minutes, or until the fish is cooked through and the topping is golden and crispy.
7. Once the cod fillets are cooked, remove them from the oven and let them rest for a few minutes before serving.
8. Serve the baked cod with herbed crumb topping hot, accompanied by your favorite side dishes such as roasted vegetables, rice, or a fresh salad.

Enjoy this delicious and flavorful dish of baked cod with herbed crumb topping, perfect for a quick and easy weeknight dinner or a special occasion meal!

Lobster Risotto with Saffron

Ingredients:

- 2 lobster tails
- 1 cup Arborio rice
- 4 cups seafood or vegetable broth
- 1/2 cup dry white wine
- 1 shallot, finely chopped
- 2 cloves garlic, minced
- 2 tablespoons olive oil
- 2 tablespoons butter
- 1/4 teaspoon saffron threads
- 1/4 cup grated Parmesan cheese
- Salt and pepper to taste
- Chopped fresh parsley for garnish

Instructions:

1. Bring a large pot of salted water to a boil. Add the lobster tails and boil for about 5-7 minutes, or until the shells turn bright red and the meat is opaque and cooked through. Remove the lobster tails from the water and let them cool slightly. Once cooled, remove the meat from the shells and chop it into bite-sized pieces. Set aside.
2. In a small bowl, steep the saffron threads in 1/4 cup of hot water for about 10 minutes, or until the water turns golden yellow.
3. In a separate saucepan, heat the seafood or vegetable broth over medium heat until warm. Keep it warm while you prepare the risotto.
4. In a large skillet or Dutch oven, heat the olive oil and butter over medium heat. Add the chopped shallot and minced garlic, and sauté for 2-3 minutes, or until softened and fragrant.
5. Add the Arborio rice to the skillet and stir to coat it with the oil and butter. Cook for 1-2 minutes, stirring constantly, until the rice becomes translucent around the edges.
6. Pour in the white wine and cook, stirring constantly, until the wine is absorbed by the rice.
7. Begin adding the warm broth to the rice, one ladleful at a time, stirring constantly and allowing each addition to be absorbed before adding more. Continue this

process until the rice is creamy and tender, but still slightly firm to the bite. This should take about 18-20 minutes.
8. Once the risotto is cooked to your desired consistency, stir in the chopped lobster meat and the saffron-infused water. Cook for an additional 1-2 minutes, or until the lobster is heated through and the risotto is a vibrant yellow color.
9. Remove the skillet from the heat and stir in the grated Parmesan cheese. Season with salt and pepper to taste.
10. Serve the lobster risotto hot, garnished with chopped fresh parsley.

Enjoy this decadent and flavorful lobster risotto with saffron as a show-stopping main course for your next special occasion!

Icelandic Meat Pie

Ingredients:

For the Pastry:

- 2 1/2 cups all-purpose flour
- 1 teaspoon salt
- 1 cup unsalted butter, chilled and cubed
- 6-8 tablespoons ice water

For the Filling:

- 500g ground beef or lamb
- 1 onion, finely chopped
- 2 cloves garlic, minced
- 2 carrots, diced
- 1 celery stalk, diced
- 1/2 cup frozen peas
- 1 tablespoon tomato paste
- 1 tablespoon Worcestershire sauce
- 1 teaspoon dried thyme
- Salt and pepper to taste
- 1 egg, beaten (for egg wash)

Instructions:

1. Preheat your oven to 200°C (400°F).
2. In a large bowl, whisk together the flour and salt. Add the chilled, cubed butter and use a pastry cutter or your fingertips to work the butter into the flour until the mixture resembles coarse crumbs.
3. Gradually add the ice water, 1 tablespoon at a time, mixing with a fork until the dough comes together into a rough ball. Be careful not to overwork the dough. If it's too dry, add a little more water.
4. Divide the dough into two equal portions, shape each into a disk, wrap them in plastic wrap, and refrigerate for at least 30 minutes.

5. While the dough is chilling, prepare the filling. In a large skillet, cook the ground beef or lamb over medium heat until browned and cooked through, breaking it up with a spoon as it cooks.
6. Add the chopped onion, minced garlic, diced carrots, and diced celery to the skillet. Cook, stirring occasionally, until the vegetables are softened, about 5-6 minutes.
7. Stir in the frozen peas, tomato paste, Worcestershire sauce, dried thyme, salt, and pepper. Cook for another 2-3 minutes, until the peas are heated through and the filling is well combined. Remove from heat and let cool slightly.
8. On a lightly floured surface, roll out one portion of the chilled pastry dough into a circle large enough to line the bottom and sides of a pie dish. Transfer the rolled-out dough to the pie dish and gently press it into place.
9. Spoon the meat filling into the pastry-lined pie dish, spreading it out evenly.
10. Roll out the remaining portion of chilled pastry dough into a circle large enough to cover the pie. Place it over the filling and trim any excess dough from the edges. Crimp the edges to seal the pie.
11. Brush the top of the pie with the beaten egg to create a golden crust.
12. Use a sharp knife to cut a few slits in the top of the pie to allow steam to escape during baking.
13. Place the pie in the preheated oven and bake for 30-35 minutes, or until the crust is golden brown and the filling is bubbling.
14. Remove the pie from the oven and let it cool for a few minutes before slicing and serving.

Enjoy this comforting and flavorful Icelandic meat pie as a delicious main course for a cozy meal!

Grilled Arctic Char with Mustard-Dill Sauce

Ingredients:

For the Grilled Arctic Char:

- 4 Arctic char fillets (about 150-200g each), skin-on
- Salt and pepper to taste
- Olive oil, for brushing

For the Mustard-Dill Sauce:

- 1/2 cup mayonnaise
- 2 tablespoons Dijon mustard
- 1 tablespoon fresh dill, chopped
- 1 tablespoon lemon juice
- 1 teaspoon honey
- Salt and pepper to taste

Instructions:

1. Preheat your grill to medium-high heat.
2. Season the Arctic char fillets with salt and pepper on both sides.
3. Brush the grill grates with olive oil to prevent sticking.
4. Place the Arctic char fillets on the grill, skin-side down. Grill for about 4-5 minutes on each side, or until the fish is cooked through and flakes easily with a fork. The skin should be crispy and charred.
5. While the fish is grilling, prepare the mustard-dill sauce. In a small bowl, combine the mayonnaise, Dijon mustard, chopped fresh dill, lemon juice, honey, salt, and pepper. Mix until well combined. Taste and adjust seasoning if needed.
6. Once the Arctic char fillets are grilled to perfection, remove them from the grill and transfer them to a serving platter.
7. Serve the grilled Arctic char hot, accompanied by the mustard-dill sauce on the side.
8. Garnish with additional fresh dill if desired.
9. Enjoy this flavorful and succulent grilled Arctic char with mustard-dill sauce as a delicious main course!

This dish pairs well with roasted potatoes, steamed vegetables, or a fresh green salad.

It's perfect for a summer barbecue or a special dinner with friends and family.

Smoked Trout Salad with Horseradish Dressing

Ingredients:

For the Salad:

- 200g smoked trout fillets, flaked
- 4 cups mixed salad greens (such as arugula, spinach, and lettuce)
- 1/2 cucumber, thinly sliced
- 1/2 red onion, thinly sliced
- 1/4 cup cherry tomatoes, halved
- 1/4 cup toasted walnuts or almonds
- 2 tablespoons chopped fresh dill
- Lemon wedges, for serving (optional)

For the Horseradish Dressing:

- 1/4 cup mayonnaise
- 2 tablespoons Greek yogurt (or sour cream)
- 1 tablespoon prepared horseradish
- 1 tablespoon lemon juice
- 1 teaspoon Dijon mustard
- Salt and pepper to taste

Instructions:

1. In a large mixing bowl, combine the mixed salad greens, sliced cucumber, sliced red onion, halved cherry tomatoes, toasted walnuts or almonds, and chopped fresh dill.
2. Add the flaked smoked trout to the salad bowl and gently toss everything together to combine.
3. In a small bowl, whisk together the mayonnaise, Greek yogurt (or sour cream), prepared horseradish, lemon juice, Dijon mustard, salt, and pepper until smooth and well combined. Taste and adjust seasoning if needed.
4. Drizzle the horseradish dressing over the smoked trout salad and toss gently to coat the salad ingredients evenly with the dressing.
5. Transfer the smoked trout salad to serving plates or a large serving platter.

6. Serve the salad immediately, garnished with additional chopped fresh dill and lemon wedges on the side if desired.
7. Enjoy this delicious and refreshing smoked trout salad with horseradish dressing as a light and flavorful main course or appetizer!

This salad is perfect for lunch or dinner, and it's sure to impress your guests with its vibrant colors and bold flavors. Feel free to customize the salad with your favorite greens, vegetables, and nuts for added variety and texture.

Icelandic Lamb Skewers with Yogurt-Dill Sauce

Ingredients:

For the Lamb Skewers:

- 1 lb (450g) lamb meat, cubed
- 1 red onion, cut into chunks
- 1 bell pepper, cut into chunks
- Salt and pepper to taste
- Olive oil for brushing

For the Yogurt-Dill Sauce:

- 1 cup Greek yogurt
- 2 tablespoons chopped fresh dill
- 1 clove garlic, minced
- 1 tablespoon lemon juice
- Salt and pepper to taste

Instructions:

1. Prepare the Lamb Skewers:
    - If you're using wooden skewers, soak them in water for at least 30 minutes to prevent burning.
    - Thread the lamb cubes onto the skewers, alternating with pieces of onion and bell pepper.
    - Season the skewers with salt and pepper, and brush them lightly with olive oil.
2. Preheat the Grill:
    - Preheat your grill to medium-high heat.
3. Grill the Skewers:
    - Place the skewers on the preheated grill and cook for about 8-10 minutes, turning occasionally, or until the lamb is cooked to your desired level of doneness and the vegetables are tender and slightly charred.
4. Make the Yogurt-Dill Sauce:
    - In a small bowl, mix together the Greek yogurt, chopped dill, minced garlic, lemon juice, salt, and pepper. Adjust seasoning to taste.
5. Serve:
    - Once the skewers are done, remove them from the grill and let them rest for a few minutes.

- Serve the lamb skewers hot with the yogurt-dill sauce on the side for dipping.
6. Enjoy!
    - Enjoy your Icelandic Lamb Skewers with Yogurt-Dill Sauce as a delicious and satisfying meal!

Feel free to adjust the seasoning and ingredients according to your taste preferences.

Enjoy your culinary adventure!

Pan-Fried Haddock with Lemon-Caper Sauce

Ingredients:

For the Pan-Fried Haddock:

- 4 haddock fillets
- Salt and pepper to taste
- 1/2 cup all-purpose flour
- 2 tablespoons olive oil
- 2 tablespoons butter
- Lemon wedges for serving

For the Lemon-Caper Sauce:

- 2 tablespoons butter
- 2 cloves garlic, minced
- 2 tablespoons capers, drained
- 1/4 cup dry white wine
- Juice of 1 lemon
- 1/4 cup chicken or vegetable broth
- Salt and pepper to taste
- 2 tablespoons chopped fresh parsley (optional, for garnish)

Instructions:

1. Prepare the Haddock:
    - Pat the haddock fillets dry with paper towels. Season both sides with salt and pepper.
    - Dredge each fillet in flour, shaking off any excess.
2. Pan-Fry the Haddock:
    - In a large skillet, heat the olive oil and butter over medium-high heat.
    - Once the butter has melted and the skillet is hot, add the haddock fillets in a single layer.
    - Cook the fillets for about 3-4 minutes on each side, or until they are golden brown and cooked through. The cooking time may vary depending on the thickness of the fillets. Be careful not to overcook.
3. Make the Lemon-Caper Sauce:
    - In the same skillet used for cooking the haddock, melt the butter over medium heat.
    - Add the minced garlic and cook for about 1 minute, or until fragrant.

- Stir in the capers, white wine, lemon juice, and broth. Allow the mixture to simmer for 2-3 minutes, or until slightly reduced.
- Season the sauce with salt and pepper to taste.

4. Serve:
   - Transfer the cooked haddock fillets to serving plates.
   - Spoon the lemon-caper sauce over the fillets.
   - Garnish with chopped fresh parsley, if desired.
   - Serve hot with lemon wedges on the side.

5. Enjoy!
   - Enjoy your Pan-Fried Haddock with Lemon-Caper Sauce as a flavorful and elegant seafood dish!

Feel free to adjust the seasoning and ingredients according to your taste preferences.

Serve the haddock with your favorite side dishes, such as roasted vegetables or a fresh salad, for a complete meal. Bon appétit!

Langoustine Pasta with Garlic and Parsley

Ingredients:

- 1 lb (450g) langoustine tails, peeled and deveined
- 8 oz (225g) linguine or spaghetti
- 4 cloves garlic, minced
- 1/4 cup fresh parsley, chopped
- 1/4 cup extra virgin olive oil
- Salt and pepper to taste
- Red pepper flakes (optional)
- Grated Parmesan cheese for serving

Instructions:

1. Cook the Pasta:
    - Bring a large pot of salted water to a boil.
    - Add the linguine or spaghetti and cook according to package instructions until al dente.
    - Reserve about 1/2 cup of pasta water, then drain the pasta and set aside.
2. Prepare the Langoustine:
    - Heat a large skillet over medium heat and add the olive oil.
    - Add the minced garlic and cook for about 1 minute until fragrant, being careful not to burn it.
    - Add the langoustine tails to the skillet and cook for 2-3 minutes until they are pink and cooked through.
    - Season with salt, pepper, and red pepper flakes if using.
3. Combine the Pasta and Langoustine:
    - Add the cooked pasta to the skillet with the langoustine.
    - Toss everything together gently, adding some of the reserved pasta water if needed to loosen the sauce and coat the pasta evenly.
4. Add Parsley and Serve:
    - Stir in the chopped parsley and continue to cook for another minute until the parsley is wilted and incorporated.
    - Taste and adjust seasoning if necessary.
5. Serve:
    - Divide the langoustine pasta among serving plates.
    - Garnish with additional chopped parsley and grated Parmesan cheese if desired.
    - Serve immediately, accompanied by crusty bread or a side salad.

6. Enjoy!
    - Enjoy your flavorful langoustine pasta with garlic and parsley!

Feel free to customize this recipe by adding other ingredients like cherry tomatoes, white wine, or lemon zest for extra flavor. It's a versatile dish that can be easily adapted to suit your taste preferences. Buon appetito!

Lamb Meatballs in Tomato Sauce

Ingredients:

For the Lamb Meatballs:

- 1 lb (450g) ground lamb
- 1/2 cup breadcrumbs
- 1/4 cup grated Parmesan cheese
- 2 cloves garlic, minced
- 1 egg, lightly beaten
- 2 tablespoons chopped fresh parsley
- 1 teaspoon dried oregano
- Salt and pepper to taste

For the Tomato Sauce:

- 2 tablespoons olive oil
- 1 onion, finely chopped
- 2 cloves garlic, minced
- 1 can (14 oz / 400g) crushed tomatoes
- 1 tablespoon tomato paste
- 1 teaspoon sugar (optional, to balance acidity)
- 1 teaspoon dried basil
- Salt and pepper to taste
- Chopped fresh basil or parsley for garnish

Instructions:

1. Prepare the Lamb Meatballs:
    - In a large bowl, combine the ground lamb, breadcrumbs, Parmesan cheese, minced garlic, beaten egg, chopped parsley, dried oregano, salt, and pepper.
    - Mix until all ingredients are well combined.
    - Shape the mixture into meatballs, about 1 to 1.5 inches in diameter, and set aside.
2. Cook the Tomato Sauce:
    - In a large skillet or saucepan, heat the olive oil over medium heat.
    - Add the finely chopped onion and cook until softened and translucent, about 5 minutes.
    - Add the minced garlic and cook for an additional minute until fragrant.
    - Stir in the crushed tomatoes, tomato paste, sugar (if using), dried basil, salt, and pepper.
    - Bring the sauce to a simmer and let it cook for about 10-15 minutes, stirring occasionally, until slightly thickened.
3. Cook the Lamb Meatballs:

- While the sauce is simmering, heat a separate skillet over medium heat and add a bit of olive oil.
- Add the lamb meatballs to the skillet in a single layer, making sure not to overcrowd the pan.
- Cook the meatballs for about 8-10 minutes, turning occasionally, until browned on all sides and cooked through.

4. Combine Meatballs with Sauce:
    - Once the meatballs are cooked, transfer them to the simmering tomato sauce.
    - Gently stir to coat the meatballs in the sauce.
    - Let the meatballs simmer in the sauce for an additional 5 minutes to allow the flavors to meld together.
5. Serve:
    - Serve the lamb meatballs and tomato sauce hot, garnished with chopped fresh basil or parsley.
    - Enjoy as is or serve over cooked pasta, rice, or with crusty bread.
6. Enjoy!
    - Enjoy your delicious lamb meatballs in tomato sauce!

Feel free to adjust the seasoning and ingredients according to your taste preferences. This dish is also great with a sprinkle of grated Parmesan cheese on top before serving. Buon appetito!

Baked Salmon with Roasted Vegetables

Ingredients:

- 4 salmon fillets
- 2 tablespoons olive oil
- 2 cloves garlic, minced
- 1 tablespoon lemon juice
- 1 teaspoon dried thyme
- Salt and pepper to taste

For the Roasted Vegetables:

- 2 cups mixed vegetables (such as bell peppers, zucchini, carrots, and cherry tomatoes), chopped into bite-sized pieces
- 2 tablespoons olive oil
- 1 teaspoon dried Italian herbs (or your choice of herbs)
- Salt and pepper to taste

Instructions:

1. Preheat the Oven:
    - Preheat your oven to 400°F (200°C).
2. Prepare the Salmon:
    - In a small bowl, whisk together the olive oil, minced garlic, lemon juice, dried thyme, salt, and pepper.
    - Place the salmon fillets in a baking dish lined with parchment paper or lightly greased.
    - Brush the salmon fillets with the olive oil mixture, coating them evenly.
3. Prepare the Roasted Vegetables:
    - In a separate bowl, toss the chopped mixed vegetables with olive oil, dried herbs, salt, and pepper until well coated.
    - Spread the vegetables in a single layer on a baking sheet lined with parchment paper.
4. Bake:
    - Place both the baking dish with salmon and the baking sheet with vegetables in the preheated oven.
    - Bake for about 15-20 minutes, or until the salmon is cooked through and flakes easily with a fork, and the vegetables are tender and slightly caramelized. The cooking time may vary depending on the thickness of the salmon fillets and the type of vegetables used.

5. Serve:
    - Once done, remove the salmon and roasted vegetables from the oven.
    - Serve the baked salmon hot alongside the roasted vegetables.
    - Optionally, garnish the salmon with fresh herbs or a squeeze of lemon juice before serving.
6. Enjoy!
    - Enjoy your delicious and healthy baked salmon with roasted vegetables!

Feel free to customize this recipe by using your favorite vegetables or adding additional seasonings and herbs to suit your taste preferences. It's a versatile dish that's perfect for a quick and nutritious weeknight dinner. Bon appétit!

Icelandic Fish Soup

Ingredients:

- 1 lb (450g) white fish fillets (such as cod, haddock, or pollock), cut into bite-sized pieces
- 2 large potatoes, peeled and diced
- 1 onion, finely chopped
- 2 tablespoons butter
- 2 tablespoons all-purpose flour
- 3 cups fish or vegetable broth
- 1 cup whole milk or cream
- Salt and pepper to taste
- Chopped fresh parsley for garnish

Instructions:

1. Prepare the Ingredients:
    - Cut the fish fillets into bite-sized pieces and set aside.
    - Peel and dice the potatoes, and finely chop the onion.
2. Cook the Potatoes and Onions:
    - In a large pot, melt the butter over medium heat.
    - Add the chopped onions and cook until softened and translucent, about 5 minutes.
    - Add the diced potatoes to the pot and cook for another 5 minutes, stirring occasionally.
3. Make the Roux:
    - Sprinkle the flour over the cooked onions and potatoes, stirring to coat evenly.
    - Cook for 1-2 minutes to allow the flour to cook slightly and eliminate the raw flour taste.
4. Add Broth and Simmer:
    - Gradually pour in the fish or vegetable broth while stirring constantly to prevent lumps from forming.
    - Bring the mixture to a simmer and cook for about 10-15 minutes, or until the potatoes are tender and cooked through.
5. Add Fish and Milk:
    - Once the potatoes are cooked, add the bite-sized fish pieces to the pot.
    - Pour in the whole milk or cream, stirring gently to combine.

- Let the soup simmer for an additional 5-7 minutes, or until the fish is cooked through and flakes easily with a fork. Be careful not to overcook the fish.
6. Season and Serve:
    - Season the soup with salt and pepper to taste, adjusting as needed.
    - Ladle the Icelandic fish soup into serving bowls and garnish with chopped fresh parsley.
    - Serve hot, accompanied by crusty bread or crackers if desired.
7. Enjoy!
    - Enjoy your delicious Icelandic fish soup, a comforting and traditional dish perfect for a chilly day!

Feel free to customize this recipe by adding other ingredients such as carrots, celery, or leeks for extra flavor and texture. You can also adjust the consistency of the soup by adding more broth or milk to your liking. Bon appétit!

Lamb Loin Chops with Red Wine Sauce

Ingredients:

For the Lamb Loin Chops:

- 4 lamb loin chops
- Salt and pepper to taste
- 2 tablespoons olive oil
- 2 cloves garlic, minced
- 1 teaspoon dried rosemary (or 1 tablespoon chopped fresh rosemary)

For the Red Wine Sauce:

- 1 cup red wine (such as Cabernet Sauvignon or Merlot)
- 1/2 cup beef or lamb broth
- 1 tablespoon butter
- 1 shallot, finely chopped
- 2 cloves garlic, minced
- 1 teaspoon dried thyme (or 1 tablespoon chopped fresh thyme)
- Salt and pepper to taste

Instructions:

1. Prepare the Lamb Loin Chops:
    - Pat the lamb loin chops dry with paper towels.
    - Season both sides of the chops generously with salt, pepper, and dried rosemary.
2. Sear the Lamb Loin Chops:
    - Heat olive oil in a large skillet over medium-high heat.
    - Once the skillet is hot, add the lamb loin chops and sear for 3-4 minutes on each side, or until they are browned and caramelized on the outside but still pink in the center (for medium-rare). Adjust cooking time according to your desired level of doneness.
    - Transfer the seared chops to a plate and cover loosely with foil to keep warm.
3. Make the Red Wine Sauce:
    - In the same skillet used to cook the lamb, add the chopped shallot and minced garlic. Cook for 2-3 minutes, or until softened and fragrant.
    - Pour in the red wine and beef or lamb broth, scraping the bottom of the skillet to deglaze and loosen any browned bits.

- Stir in the dried thyme and season the sauce with salt and pepper to taste.
- Allow the sauce to simmer and reduce by half, stirring occasionally, for about 5-7 minutes.
4. Finish the Sauce:
    - Once the sauce has reduced, remove the skillet from the heat and stir in the butter until it melts and the sauce becomes glossy.
5. Serve:
    - Place the seared lamb loin chops on serving plates.
    - Spoon the red wine sauce over the chops.
    - Garnish with fresh herbs like chopped parsley or thyme, if desired.
6. Enjoy!
    - Serve your lamb loin chops with red wine sauce immediately, alongside your favorite side dishes like roasted vegetables, mashed potatoes, or a simple green salad.

This dish is sure to impress with its rich flavors and elegant presentation. Enjoy your culinary creation!

Grilled Prawns with Mango Salsa

Ingredients:

For the Grilled Prawns:

- 1 lb (450g) large prawns, peeled and deveined
- 2 tablespoons olive oil
- 2 cloves garlic, minced
- 1 teaspoon paprika
- Salt and pepper to taste
- Wooden or metal skewers (if using wooden skewers, soak them in water for 30 minutes before grilling)

For the Mango Salsa:

- 2 ripe mangoes, peeled, pitted, and diced
- 1/2 red onion, finely chopped
- 1 red bell pepper, diced
- 1 jalapeño pepper, seeded and finely chopped (optional, for heat)
- Juice of 1 lime
- 2 tablespoons chopped fresh cilantro
- Salt and pepper to taste

Instructions:

1. Marinate the Prawns:
    - In a bowl, combine the prawns with olive oil, minced garlic, paprika, salt, and pepper. Toss until the prawns are evenly coated. Allow them to marinate for at least 15-30 minutes in the refrigerator.
2. Prepare the Mango Salsa:
    - In a separate bowl, combine the diced mangoes, finely chopped red onion, diced red bell pepper, chopped jalapeño pepper (if using), lime juice, chopped cilantro, salt, and pepper. Mix well to combine. Taste and adjust seasoning as needed. Refrigerate until ready to serve.
3. Grill the Prawns:
    - Preheat your grill to medium-high heat.
    - Thread the marinated prawns onto skewers, dividing them evenly.
    - Place the prawn skewers on the preheated grill and cook for 2-3 minutes on each side, or until they are pink and opaque, and have grill marks. Be careful not to overcook the prawns, as they can become rubbery.

4. Serve:
   - Once the prawns are cooked, remove them from the grill and transfer them to a serving platter.
   - Serve the grilled prawns hot, accompanied by the mango salsa on the side.
5. Enjoy!
   - Enjoy your grilled prawns with mango salsa as a delicious appetizer or main course! The combination of sweet mango salsa and succulent grilled prawns is sure to be a hit at any gathering.

Feel free to adjust the seasoning and ingredients in the mango salsa according to your taste preferences. You can also customize the level of heat by adding more or less jalapeño pepper. Bon appétit!

Arctic Char Fillets with Lemon-Herb Butter

Ingredients:

For the Arctic Char Fillets:

- 4 Arctic char fillets, skin-on
- Salt and pepper to taste
- Olive oil for drizzling

For the Lemon-Herb Butter:

- 1/2 cup (1 stick) unsalted butter, softened
- Zest of 1 lemon
- 2 tablespoons fresh lemon juice
- 2 tablespoons chopped fresh herbs (such as parsley, dill, or chives)
- 2 cloves garlic, minced
- Salt and pepper to taste

Instructions:

1. Preheat the Oven:
    - Preheat your oven to 400°F (200°C).
2. Prepare the Lemon-Herb Butter:
    - In a small bowl, combine the softened butter, lemon zest, lemon juice, chopped fresh herbs, minced garlic, salt, and pepper. Mix until well combined. Set aside.
3. Prepare the Arctic Char Fillets:
    - Pat the Arctic char fillets dry with paper towels.
    - Season both sides of the fillets with salt and pepper.
4. Cook the Fillets:
    - Place the seasoned Arctic char fillets skin-side down on a baking sheet lined with parchment paper or aluminum foil.
    - Drizzle the fillets lightly with olive oil.
    - Place small dollops of the lemon-herb butter on top of each fillet.
5. Bake:
    - Transfer the baking sheet to the preheated oven and bake the Arctic char fillets for 12-15 minutes, or until the fish is cooked through and flakes easily with a fork. The cooking time may vary depending on the thickness of the fillets.
6. Serve:

- Once done, remove the Arctic char fillets from the oven.
- Serve the fillets hot, accompanied by additional lemon wedges and any remaining lemon-herb butter on the side.

7. Enjoy!
   - Enjoy your delicious Arctic char fillets with lemon-herb butter as a main course. The buttery, citrusy flavor complements the delicate taste of the fish perfectly.

Feel free to serve the Arctic char fillets with your favorite side dishes, such as roasted vegetables, rice, or a fresh salad, for a complete and satisfying meal. Bon appétit!

Lamb Shoulder Slow Cooked in Stout

Ingredients:

- 1 (4-5 lb) lamb shoulder, bone-in
- Salt and pepper to taste
- 2 tablespoons olive oil
- 2 onions, sliced
- 4 cloves garlic, minced
- 2 carrots, chopped
- 2 stalks celery, chopped
- 2 cups stout beer
- 2 cups beef or lamb broth
- 2 bay leaves
- 2 sprigs fresh rosemary
- 2 sprigs fresh thyme

Instructions:

1. Prepare the Lamb Shoulder:
    - Season the lamb shoulder generously with salt and pepper on all sides.
2. Sear the Lamb Shoulder:
    - Heat the olive oil in a large skillet or Dutch oven over medium-high heat.
    - Sear the lamb shoulder on all sides until browned, about 4-5 minutes per side. This step helps to develop flavor and seal in juices.
3. Prepare the Slow Cooker:
    - Transfer the seared lamb shoulder to the slow cooker.
    - Add the sliced onions, minced garlic, chopped carrots, and celery around the lamb shoulder.
4. Add Liquid and Herbs:
    - Pour the stout beer and beef or lamb broth over the lamb shoulder and vegetables in the slow cooker.
    - Add the bay leaves, fresh rosemary, and fresh thyme sprigs to the slow cooker.
5. Cook on Low Heat:
    - Cover the slow cooker and cook the lamb shoulder on low heat for 8-10 hours, or until the meat is tender and falls off the bone easily.
6. Serve:
    - Once the lamb shoulder is cooked, carefully remove it from the slow cooker and transfer it to a serving platter.

- Allow the lamb shoulder to rest for a few minutes before slicing or shredding it.
- Serve the lamb shoulder with the cooked vegetables and strained cooking liquid as a sauce.

7. Enjoy!
    - Serve your slow-cooked lamb shoulder with stout alongside mashed potatoes, roasted vegetables, or crusty bread for a comforting and delicious meal.

This dish is perfect for a cozy night in, and the tender, flavorful meat will be sure to impress your guests. Enjoy!

Pan-Seared Cod with Garlic Butter

Ingredients:

- 4 cod fillets, about 6 oz each
- Salt and pepper to taste
- 2 tablespoons olive oil
- 4 tablespoons unsalted butter
- 4 cloves garlic, minced
- 2 tablespoons chopped fresh parsley
- 1 tablespoon lemon juice
- Lemon wedges for serving

Instructions:

1. Season the Cod Fillets:
    - Pat the cod fillets dry with paper towels.
    - Season both sides of the fillets generously with salt and pepper.
2. Heat the Olive Oil:
    - Heat the olive oil in a large skillet over medium-high heat until hot but not smoking.
3. Pan-Sear the Cod:
    - Carefully place the seasoned cod fillets in the skillet, skin side down if they have skin.
    - Cook the fillets for 3-4 minutes on each side, or until they are golden brown and cooked through. The cooking time may vary depending on the thickness of the fillets. The fish is done when it flakes easily with a fork.
4. Make the Garlic Butter Sauce:
    - While the cod is cooking, melt the unsalted butter in a small saucepan over medium heat.
    - Add the minced garlic to the melted butter and cook for 1-2 minutes, stirring frequently, until fragrant and lightly golden.
    - Stir in the chopped fresh parsley and lemon juice, then remove the saucepan from the heat.
5. Serve:
    - Once the cod fillets are cooked, transfer them to serving plates.
    - Spoon the garlic butter sauce over the cod fillets.
    - Garnish with additional chopped parsley and serve with lemon wedges on the side.
6. Enjoy!

- Serve your pan-seared cod with garlic butter hot, accompanied by your favorite side dishes such as steamed vegetables, rice, or a fresh salad.

This dish is quick and easy to make but impressive enough for a special dinner. The combination of tender cod and flavorful garlic butter sauce is sure to be a hit!

Icelandic Fish Sticks with Tartar Sauce

Ingredients:

For the Fish Sticks:

- 1 lb (450g) white fish fillets (such as cod, haddock, or pollock), cut into strips
- 1 cup all-purpose flour
- 2 eggs, beaten
- 1 cup breadcrumbs
- Salt and pepper to taste
- Cooking oil (for frying)

For the Tartar Sauce:

- 1/2 cup mayonnaise
- 2 tablespoons chopped pickles or cornichons
- 1 tablespoon capers, chopped
- 1 tablespoon fresh lemon juice
- 1 teaspoon Dijon mustard
- 1 teaspoon chopped fresh dill (optional)
- Salt and pepper to taste

Instructions:

1. Prepare the Tartar Sauce:
    - In a small bowl, combine the mayonnaise, chopped pickles, capers, lemon juice, Dijon mustard, and chopped fresh dill (if using). Mix well until all ingredients are evenly incorporated. Season with salt and pepper to taste. Cover and refrigerate until ready to serve.
2. Prepare the Fish Sticks:
    - Season the fish strips with salt and pepper.
    - Set up a breading station with three shallow bowls: one containing flour, one containing beaten eggs, and one containing breadcrumbs.
    - Dredge each fish strip in the flour, shaking off any excess.
    - Dip the floured fish strip into the beaten eggs, allowing any excess to drip off.
    - Coat the fish strip evenly with breadcrumbs, pressing gently to adhere.
3. Fry the Fish Sticks:
    - Heat cooking oil in a large skillet or frying pan over medium-high heat.

- Once the oil is hot, add the breaded fish strips in batches, being careful not to overcrowd the pan.
- Fry the fish sticks for 3-4 minutes on each side, or until they are golden brown and crispy. Use tongs to carefully flip them halfway through cooking.
- Transfer the cooked fish sticks to a plate lined with paper towels to drain any excess oil.

4. Serve:
    - Serve the hot fish sticks with the prepared tartar sauce on the side for dipping.
    - Optionally, garnish with fresh lemon wedges and chopped parsley for extra flavor and presentation.
5. Enjoy!
    - Enjoy your homemade Icelandic fish sticks with tartar sauce as a tasty and satisfying meal or appetizer!

Feel free to adjust the seasonings and ingredients in the tartar sauce according to your taste preferences. You can also customize the breading by adding herbs or spices to the breadcrumbs for extra flavor.

Baked Trout with Almond Crust

Ingredients:

- 4 trout fillets
- Salt and pepper to taste
- 1/2 cup almonds, finely chopped or ground
- 1/4 cup breadcrumbs
- 2 tablespoons grated Parmesan cheese
- 1 tablespoon chopped fresh parsley
- 1 tablespoon melted butter or olive oil
- Lemon wedges for serving

Instructions:

1. Preheat the Oven:
    - Preheat your oven to 400°F (200°C). Grease a baking dish with cooking spray or olive oil.
2. Prepare the Trout Fillets:
    - Pat the trout fillets dry with paper towels.
    - Season both sides of the fillets with salt and pepper to taste.
3. Make the Almond Crust:
    - In a shallow bowl, combine the finely chopped or ground almonds, breadcrumbs, grated Parmesan cheese, chopped fresh parsley, and melted butter or olive oil. Mix well until all ingredients are evenly incorporated.
4. Coat the Trout Fillets:
    - Dip each trout fillet into the almond mixture, coating both sides evenly. Press gently to adhere the crust to the fillets.
5. Bake the Trout:
    - Place the coated trout fillets in the prepared baking dish.
    - Bake in the preheated oven for 12-15 minutes, or until the fish is cooked through and the almond crust is golden brown and crispy.
6. Serve:
    - Once the trout fillets are baked, remove them from the oven.
    - Serve the baked trout hot, accompanied by lemon wedges for squeezing over the fish.
7. Enjoy!

- Enjoy your baked trout with almond crust as a flavorful and healthy main course! Serve it with your favorite side dishes such as steamed vegetables, rice, or a fresh salad.

This dish is quick and easy to make but impressive enough for a special dinner. The almond crust adds a crunchy texture and nutty flavor to the tender trout fillets. Bon appétit!

Lamb Burgers with Blue Cheese

Ingredients:

- 1 lb ground lamb
- 1/4 cup breadcrumbs
- 1 egg
- 2 cloves garlic, minced
- 1 tablespoon chopped fresh parsley
- Salt and pepper to taste
- 4 hamburger buns
- 4 oz blue cheese, crumbled
- Lettuce leaves
- Sliced tomatoes
- Sliced red onion
- Optional toppings: mayonnaise, mustard, ketchup

Instructions:

1. Prepare the Lamb Patties:
    - In a large mixing bowl, combine the ground lamb, breadcrumbs, egg, minced garlic, chopped parsley, salt, and pepper. Mix until well combined.
    - Divide the mixture into 4 equal portions and shape each portion into a patty, about 1/2 to 3/4 inch thick.
2. Cook the Lamb Patties:
    - Heat a grill or skillet over medium-high heat.
    - Cook the lamb patties for 4-5 minutes on each side, or until they reach your desired level of doneness. Lamb burgers are best cooked to medium (about 160°F or 71°C internal temperature), but you can adjust the cooking time according to your preference.
3. Melt the Blue Cheese:
    - During the last minute of cooking, top each lamb patty with a portion of crumbled blue cheese. Cover the grill or skillet to allow the cheese to melt slightly.
4. Assemble the Burgers:
    - Toast the hamburger buns lightly on the grill or in a toaster.
    - Place a lettuce leaf on the bottom half of each bun, followed by a lamb patty topped with melted blue cheese.
    - Add sliced tomatoes and red onion on top of the cheese.

- Spread mayonnaise, mustard, or ketchup on the top half of each bun if desired.
- Place the top half of the bun over the toppings to complete the burgers.
5. Serve:
    - Serve the lamb burgers with blue cheese immediately, alongside your favorite side dishes such as french fries, sweet potato fries, or a green salad.
6. Enjoy!
    - Enjoy your delicious lamb burgers with blue cheese, savoring the juicy lamb patties and tangy blue cheese flavor.

These lamb burgers are sure to be a hit at your next barbecue or casual dinner gathering. Customize them with your preferred toppings and enjoy!

Grilled Langoustines with Lemon and Parsley

Ingredients:

- 8-12 langoustines (also known as Dublin Bay prawns or Norway lobsters)
- 2 tablespoons olive oil
- Salt and pepper to taste
- 2-3 cloves garlic, minced
- Zest of 1 lemon
- Juice of 1 lemon
- 2 tablespoons chopped fresh parsley
- Lemon wedges for serving

Instructions:

1. Prepare the Langoustines:
    - If the langoustines are frozen, thaw them thoroughly before cooking.
    - Using kitchen shears or a sharp knife, carefully cut along the length of the langoustine shells on the underside to expose the meat.
    - Use a small knife to remove the digestive tract (the dark vein) from each langoustine.
2. Marinate the Langoustines:
    - In a bowl, combine the olive oil, minced garlic, lemon zest, lemon juice, chopped parsley, salt, and pepper. Mix well to combine.
    - Add the prepared langoustines to the bowl and toss them in the marinade until evenly coated. Let them marinate for about 15-30 minutes to allow the flavors to infuse.
3. Preheat the Grill:
    - Preheat your grill to medium-high heat. Make sure the grates are clean and lightly greased to prevent sticking.
4. Grill the Langoustines:
    - Once the grill is hot, place the langoustines directly on the grill grates, shell side down.
    - Grill the langoustines for 2-3 minutes on each side, or until the shells turn pink and the meat is opaque and slightly firm to the touch. Be careful not to overcook them, as langoustines can become tough if cooked for too long.
5. Serve:
    - Once the langoustines are cooked, remove them from the grill and transfer them to a serving platter.

- Serve the grilled langoustines hot, garnished with additional chopped parsley and lemon wedges on the side for squeezing over the langoustines.
6. Enjoy!
    - Enjoy your grilled langoustines with lemon and parsley as a flavorful appetizer or main course, alongside crusty bread and a fresh green salad.

Grilling langoustines enhances their natural sweetness and imparts a smoky flavor, while the lemon and parsley add brightness and freshness. It's a simple yet elegant dish that's perfect for summer gatherings or special occasions.

Baked Arctic Char with Lemon-Herb Crust

Ingredients:

- 4 Arctic char fillets
- Salt and pepper to taste
- 2 tablespoons olive oil
- 1 lemon, thinly sliced
- Lemon wedges (for serving)

For the Lemon-Herb Crust:

- 1/2 cup breadcrumbs (preferably panko)
- Zest of 1 lemon
- 2 tablespoons chopped fresh parsley
- 1 tablespoon chopped fresh dill
- 2 cloves garlic, minced
- Salt and pepper to taste
- 2 tablespoons melted butter

Instructions:

1. Preheat the Oven:
    - Preheat your oven to 400°F (200°C). Line a baking sheet with parchment paper or aluminum foil.
2. Prepare the Lemon-Herb Crust:
    - In a small bowl, combine the breadcrumbs, lemon zest, chopped parsley, chopped dill, minced garlic, salt, and pepper. Mix well to combine.
    - Stir in the melted butter until the mixture resembles coarse crumbs. Set aside.
3. Prepare the Arctic Char Fillets:
    - Pat the Arctic char fillets dry with paper towels.
    - Season both sides of the fillets with salt and pepper to taste.
4. Arrange the Lemon Slices:
    - Place the lemon slices in a single layer on the prepared baking sheet. This will create a bed for the Arctic char fillets and infuse them with flavor as they bake.
5. Bake the Arctic Char:
    - Place the seasoned Arctic char fillets on top of the lemon slices on the baking sheet.

- Generously coat the top of each fillet with the prepared lemon-herb crust mixture, pressing gently to adhere.
6. Bake in the Oven:
    - Transfer the baking sheet to the preheated oven and bake the Arctic char fillets for 12-15 minutes, or until the fish is cooked through and the crust is golden brown and crispy.
7. Serve:
    - Once the Arctic char fillets are baked, remove them from the oven.
    - Serve the fillets hot, accompanied by lemon wedges for squeezing over the fish.
8. Enjoy!
    - Enjoy your baked Arctic char with lemon-herb crust as a flavorful and elegant main course. Serve it with your favorite side dishes such as roasted vegetables, rice, or a fresh salad.

This dish is sure to impress with its vibrant flavors and beautiful presentation. It's perfect for a dinner party or a romantic meal at home.

Fish and Chips with Tartar Sauce

Ingredients:

For the Fish and Chips:

- 4 cod fillets, about 6 oz each
- Salt and pepper to taste
- 1 cup all-purpose flour
- 1 teaspoon baking powder
- 1 cup beer (such as lager or pale ale)
- Vegetable oil for frying
- 4 large potatoes, peeled and cut into thick fries
- Salt to taste

For the Tartar Sauce:

- 1/2 cup mayonnaise
- 2 tablespoons chopped pickles or cornichons
- 1 tablespoon capers, chopped
- 1 tablespoon fresh lemon juice
- 1 teaspoon Dijon mustard
- 1 teaspoon chopped fresh dill (optional)
- Salt and pepper to taste

Instructions:

1. Prepare the Tartar Sauce:
    - In a small bowl, combine the mayonnaise, chopped pickles, capers, lemon juice, Dijon mustard, and chopped fresh dill (if using). Mix well until all ingredients are evenly incorporated. Season with salt and pepper to taste. Cover and refrigerate until ready to serve.
2. Prepare the Fish:
    - Pat the cod fillets dry with paper towels and season them with salt and pepper on both sides.
3. Make the Batter:
    - In a mixing bowl, whisk together the all-purpose flour and baking powder. Gradually pour in the beer while whisking, until you have a smooth batter. The consistency should be similar to pancake batter.
4. Fry the Chips:
    - Heat vegetable oil in a deep fryer or large pot to 350°F (175°C).

- Fry the potato fries in batches for 5-6 minutes, or until they are golden brown and crispy. Use a slotted spoon to transfer them to a paper towel-lined plate to drain excess oil. Season with salt while they're still hot.
5. Fry the Fish:
    - Dip each cod fillet into the batter, coating it evenly.
    - Carefully lower the battered fillets into the hot oil and fry for 4-5 minutes, or until they are golden brown and crispy. You may need to fry them in batches to avoid overcrowding the fryer.
    - Transfer the fried fish to a paper towel-lined plate to drain excess oil.
6. Serve:
    - Serve the fish and chips hot, alongside the prepared tartar sauce for dipping.
7. Enjoy!
    - Enjoy your homemade fish and chips with tartar sauce, savoring the crispy exterior of the fish and the fluffy interior of the fries, along with the tangy tartar sauce.

This dish is a classic comfort food that's perfect for sharing with family and friends. Serve it with a side of malt vinegar and lemon wedges for an authentic British experience.

Slow Cooked Lamb Shanks with Root Vegetables

Ingredients:

- 4 lamb shanks
- Salt and pepper to taste
- 2 tablespoons olive oil
- 2 onions, chopped
- 4 cloves garlic, minced
- 2 carrots, peeled and chopped
- 2 parsnips, peeled and chopped
- 2 celery stalks, chopped
- 2 cups beef or vegetable broth
- 1 cup red wine (optional)
- 2 sprigs fresh rosemary
- 2 sprigs fresh thyme
- 2 bay leaves
- 1 tablespoon tomato paste
- 1 tablespoon Worcestershire sauce
- 1 tablespoon balsamic vinegar
- Chopped fresh parsley for garnish (optional)

Instructions:

1. Season the Lamb Shanks:
    - Season the lamb shanks generously with salt and pepper on all sides.
2. Brown the Lamb Shanks:
    - Heat the olive oil in a large skillet or Dutch oven over medium-high heat.
    - Brown the lamb shanks on all sides, working in batches if necessary to avoid overcrowding the pan. This step adds flavor to the dish.
3. Prepare the Slow Cooker or Dutch Oven:
    - If using a slow cooker, transfer the browned lamb shanks to the slow cooker. If using a Dutch oven, you can continue cooking in the same pot.
    - Add the chopped onions, minced garlic, carrots, parsnips, and celery to the slow cooker or Dutch oven.
4. Add Liquid and Seasonings:
    - Pour the beef or vegetable broth and red wine (if using) over the lamb shanks and vegetables.

- Add the fresh rosemary, thyme sprigs, bay leaves, tomato paste, Worcestershire sauce, and balsamic vinegar to the slow cooker or Dutch oven. These ingredients will add depth of flavor to the dish.

5. Slow Cook:
   - If using a slow cooker, cover and cook on low heat for 6-8 hours, or until the lamb is tender and falling off the bone.
   - If using a Dutch oven, cover and cook in the preheated oven at 325°F (160°C) for 3-4 hours, or until the lamb is tender.
6. Serve:
   - Once the lamb shanks are cooked, carefully remove them from the slow cooker or Dutch oven and transfer them to a serving platter.
   - Serve the lamb shanks hot, accompanied by the cooked root vegetables and some of the cooking liquid as sauce.
7. Garnish and Enjoy!
   - Garnish the lamb shanks with chopped fresh parsley if desired.
   - Enjoy your slow-cooked lamb shanks with root vegetables as a comforting and satisfying meal. Serve them with mashed potatoes, crusty bread, or a side salad for a complete dinner.

This dish is perfect for a special occasion or a cozy family dinner. The tender lamb, flavorful vegetables, and rich sauce will impress your guests and warm your soul.

Icelandic Lamb Stew with Barley

Ingredients:

- 1 lb lamb stew meat, cut into bite-sized pieces
- Salt and pepper to taste
- 2 tablespoons olive oil
- 1 onion, chopped
- 2 carrots, peeled and chopped
- 2 celery stalks, chopped
- 2 cloves garlic, minced
- 1 cup pearl barley, rinsed
- 6 cups beef or vegetable broth
- 2 bay leaves
- 2 sprigs fresh thyme
- 2 potatoes, peeled and chopped
- Chopped fresh parsley for garnish (optional)

Instructions:

1. Season the Lamb:
    - Season the lamb stew meat with salt and pepper to taste.
2. Brown the Lamb:
    - Heat the olive oil in a large pot or Dutch oven over medium-high heat.
    - Add the seasoned lamb stew meat to the pot and brown it on all sides, working in batches if necessary. This step adds flavor to the stew.
3. Saute the Vegetables:
    - Add the chopped onion, carrots, and celery to the pot with the browned lamb.
    - Cook the vegetables for 5-6 minutes, or until they begin to soften.
    - Add the minced garlic and cook for an additional 1-2 minutes, until fragrant.
4. Add the Barley and Broth:
    - Stir in the rinsed pearl barley, beef or vegetable broth, bay leaves, and fresh thyme sprigs.
    - Bring the mixture to a simmer, then reduce the heat to low and cover the pot.
5. Simmer the Stew:

- Let the stew simmer for 1-1.5 hours, stirring occasionally, or until the lamb is tender and the barley is cooked through. Add more broth if needed to reach your desired consistency.
6. Add the Potatoes:
    - Once the lamb and barley are tender, add the chopped potatoes to the pot.
    - Continue to simmer the stew for an additional 20-30 minutes, or until the potatoes are cooked through and the stew has thickened slightly.
7. Serve:
    - Once the stew is ready, remove the bay leaves and thyme sprigs.
    - Ladle the Icelandic lamb stew with barley into bowls and garnish with chopped fresh parsley if desired.
8. Enjoy!
    - Serve your hearty Icelandic lamb stew with crusty bread or a side salad for a complete and satisfying meal. Enjoy the comforting flavors of this traditional dish!

This Icelandic lamb stew with barley is sure to warm you up from the inside out and is perfect for sharing with family and friends.